JANE GOODALL

Gloria D. Miklowitz

Dominie Press, Inc.

Publisher: Raymond Yuen
Editor: John S. F. Graham
Designer: Greg DiGenti
Photo Credits: Michael Neugebauer/Jane Goodall
Institute (cover); Jane Goodall Institute (page 4);
K. Amman/Corbis (pages 13 and 17);
K.Ward/Corbis (page 20); David S. Holloway/
Jane Goodall Institute (page 24)

Text copyright © 2002 Gloria D. Miklowitz

Published by:
Dominie Press, Inc.

1949 Kellogg Avenue
Carlsbad, California 92008 USA
www.dominie.com

Paperback ISBN 0-7685-1218-2
Library Bound Edition ISBN 0-7685-1543-2
Printed in Singapore by PH Productions Pte Ltd
2 3 4 5 6 PH 04 03

Table of Contents

Jane Goodall as a child, with a toy monkey

Chapter 1

Animal Life

As a small child, Jane Goodall already had the patience and curiosity that would make her a scientist who studies animal behavior. Born April 3, 1934, in London, she lived her early years in the country in an old manor house where her father, an engineer, had grown up. There was a big farm next door.

One day, when she was 4, Jane crouched in a henhouse, curious to find out where eggs came from. It was hot and almost dark, but she could see the chicken in its nest, a few feet away. She stayed very still for a long time, watching. Finally the bird raised itself. A round, white object came from between its legs and landed on the straw. It was an egg.

Terribly excited, Jane ran home to tell her mother, who had worried about her long absence. When her mother saw the excitement in Jane's eyes, she did not scold Jane, but sat down to listen to her.

Throughout her childhood, Jane kept pets and studied any animal life she could find. From observing her dog, Rusty, she became convinced he could think and plan.

She loved books about animals and read them again and again, especially *The Jungle Book*, by Rudyard Kipling and *The Story of Doctor Dolittle*, by Hugh Lofting. Someday, she dreamed, she would go to Africa to see animals in the wild.

After high school, Jane enrolled in secretarial school. She wanted to save up enough money to go to Africa. She worked as a secretary and then at a film studio where medical films were made. She often visited the Natural History Museum in London.

But it wasn't until she was 23 years old that her dream came true. In 1956, a letter from an old school friend arrived. In the letter, her friend invited Jane to visit her family's farm in Kenya, Africa. Jane didn't have enough money for a ticket to Africa yet, but she still had a big dream of going there.

To save money, she moved back to the country and lived on the same farm where she grew up. She left her job with the film studio and went to work as a waitress at a big hotel near the farm. When she had saved up enough money, she bought a ticket to Africa.

Chapter 2

Africa

Before leaving, Jane arranged for
a job at a big company in Kenya to
support her stay. After she arrived,
someone told her, "If you are interested
in animals, you must meet Dr. Louis
Leakey." Leakey believed that the
remains of the earliest humans could

be found in Africa. Jane made an appointment to see the famous man.

Leakey's office was crowded with papers, fossil bones, teeth, stone tools, and even a cage with a tiny mouse and her six babies. Leakey was impressed by Jane's knowledge and enthusiasm and offered her a job as a secretary.

One day, as they walked together, Leakey told Jane about a group of chimpanzees living on a remote lakeshore. Leakey had been looking for years for the right person to study them. The more Leakey spoke, the more excited Jane became, but she had no qualifications for such a job. "Louis, I wish you'd stop talking about these chimps," she said, "because that's the kind of thing I've wanted to do all my life."

"Why do you think I'm talking about them?" Leakey asked.

The chimpanzees were in a 30-square-mile region of rugged country. The area was in Tanzania, bordering Lake Tanganyika. People considered it dangerous for a young woman to go into the jungle. Not Jane.

In July 1960, at the age of 26, with no special training and little funding to support her stay, Jane finally arrived at Gombe Stream Nature Reserve. (It later became the Gombe National Park.) She was accompanied by her mother, a cook, and two park rangers.

Dr. Leakey thought Jane would be good at observing chimpanzee behavior because she didn't have any expectations about what she would see.

Scientists at the time thought that chimpanzees were simple forest creatures. But Jane thought differently.

She said later that her dream was "to watch free, wild animals living their own, undisturbed lives."

As soon as she pitched her tent, Jane climbed a hill, looking for chimpanzees. The forests were lush with growth. They were almost impossible to go through, but she felt at home. Signs of life were all around her. Many different colored birds flew among the trees. There were wild pigs, bushbuck, baboons, and sometimes buffalo, as well as snakes and other animals.

In the next few weeks, Jane spent 10 to 12 hours a day waiting and watching, but she didn't see any chimpanzees. Her

Jane Goodall takes pictures of a family of chimpanzees

money was starting to run out. She and her mother got malaria. But still, she waited and watched.

Then one day, after several months, Jane climbed a peak and looked through her binoculars. Her heart raced. There they were—chimpanzees. But when they noticed her, they ran away in fear. Would she be able to get close enough to study them?

Chapter 3

Chimpanzees

Jane Goodall could hardly sleep
after seeing her first chimpanzees.
She couldn't wait for morning to
come so she could follow them.

Chimpanzees are one of the smallest
of the great apes, which include gorillas

and orangutans. They stand about 4 feet tall and weigh between 100 and 150 pounds. All have brown skin and black, coarse hair. They have large ears, small noses, a bony ridge above their brown eyes, and big lips.

Chimpanzees are considered to be the closest relative to human beings. They have hands that can grasp and eyes that move together so they can see depth. They rely on eyesight more than on smell to detect danger. They have the same blood groups as ours, and they suffer some of the same diseases, especially lung infections and intestinal disorders.

Jane hoped to learn more about these animals than she already knew. She knew getting close to them would take time. The thick forests made following them difficult. Sometimes she came face-to-face with dangerous animals. Malaria and other tropical sicknesses were a constant threat.

Jane followed the troop of chimpanzees she first saw, and later learned to look for them in trees bearing ripe fruit. For a full eight months, they would run away whenever she got within 150 feet of them. It took another six months for her to get within thirty feet.

Each morning she woke up at 5:30 and had coffee and bread for breakfast. She packed a light lunch of canned meat or a sandwich and a thermos with coffee into her knapsack. She wore tan shorts and shirts to blend into the forest and tied her blond hair into a ponytail. She always carried a notebook, pen, and binoculars. Then she set off to find the trees where the chimpanzees would be.

Jane Goodall communicates with a baby chimpanzee

Chapter 4

David Greybeard

The first chimpanzee to accept Jane Goodall was a large male. She named him David Greybeard. One evening, when she returned to camp, the cook told her that a male chimpanzee had come into the camp clearing to feed on the fruit tree growing there. The chimpanzee had also gone into Jane's tent and taken some bananas. It was David Greybeard. He returned three more times to eat nuts and bananas. A month later, when another tree bore ripe fruit, he returned and actually took a banana from Jane's hand.

Eventually, Jane gave names to all of the chimpanzees in the area. Besides David Greybeard, there was Goliath, an unusually large chimpanzee, who became an alpha male—the leader of the troop. Flo was an ugly but gentle female, whose children Jane named Faben, Figan, Flint, and Fifi. And there were many others.

From Flo, Jane learned that female chimpanzees in the wild reproduce every five to six years. Each baby would ride on Flo's back. Flo groomed them

Jane Goodall holds a chimpanzee in Gombe National Park, Tanzania

and taught them what foods to eat and how to make a nest. She would fearlessly protect her children if they were threatened.

One day, Jane observed David Greybeard at a giant red termite hill. He stuck a finger into the hill to make a small opening. He stripped a long stem of wild grass with his fingers and lips. Then he poked the stem into the hole. When he pulled out the stem it was covered with insects, which he licked off like candy. Then he stuck the stem back into the nest. She observed another chimpanzee, who she named Goliath, doing the same thing.

Another time, Jane saw a chimpanzee trying to drink water from a small hole in a tree trunk. The hole was too small for the chimpanzee's mouth to reach the water. The chimpanzee crumpled some leaves, soaked them in the water, and then sucked the water out of the leaves. These actions showed Jane that chimpanzees can reason and use simple tools to solve problems. Before she made her observations, scientists assumed that only people made and used tools. But these chimpanzees proved them wrong.

Every evening, Jane wrote in her journal what she had observed. What she wrote interested the entire world.

Chapter 5

Remarkable and Different

In 1961, the National Geographic
Society provided more money for Jane
Goodall's research. The society sent
Hugo van Lawick to Africa to photo-
graph the chimpanzees. Van Lawick
found Jane living a very frugal life with
only one knife, one fork, and one plate

Jane Goodall, founder of the Jane Goodall Institute

for eating. He brought additional supplies that would make life easier for them.

Among the many pictures Van Lawick took were ones showing chimpanzees killing and eating smaller animals and sharing their feast. Before Jane wrote about this behavior, people thought that all chimpanzees were vegetarians.

Jane and Van Lawick married in 1964. Their son, Hugo Eric Louis, nicknamed "Grub," was born in 1967. Jane modeled her behavior as a mother on Flo, carrying Grub wherever she went.

At first, Jane believed chimpanzees were kinder and gentler than humans. With time, she realized they had a dark side, too. There were incidences of adults killing infant chimpanzees. At one time, a war between chimpanzees from the north and those in the south went on until all the southern chimpanzees were killed.

After 30 years in Africa, Jane became very close to Flo's daughter Fifi. Fifi's children are Freud, Frodo, Fanni, Faustino, Flossy, Ferdinand, Fred, and Flirt. Each chimpanzee is remarkable and different in its own way.

Today, Jane travels the world, speaking about chimpanzees and the need to protect the environment for all living things. She says that all over Africa these amazing creatures, so like humans, need rescuing. Babies are sold as pets, or used in biomedical research, or for entertainment. In Burundi, where almost all the forests have been destroyed, only 4 percent of the chimpanzees are left. Urged by Jane, the president of that country agreed to set aside forest land for the remaining chimpanzees.

Jane works to improve the living conditions of chimpanzees in zoos, medical research laboratories, and other places. She is against using such close relatives to humans in research.

"It's all about respecting an individual's rights to live and enjoy certain freedoms, whether human or nonhuman," Jane says. "We all have a place in the world and we should respect that."

Further reading about Jane Goodall and her work can be found at the library or by visiting her Web site at www.janegoodall.org.

Glossary

Abounded - containing a lot of something.

Alpha - in biology, the leader of a group of the same animals.

Binoculars - two lenses attached together that let a person see far away things as if they were up close.

Burundi - a small East African country.

Bushbuck - a large African antelope.

Impenetrable - unable for someone or something to go through.

Intestinal - having to do with the intestines, or guts, of a person or animal.

Kenya - a large East African country.

Lake Tanganyika - a large lake in East Africa bordered by Burundi, Rwanda, Tanzania, The Democratic Republic of the Congo (formerly Zaire), and Zambia.

Malaria - a tropical disease caused by mosquito bites. It used to be fatal almost all the time, but doctors can treat it now with antibiotics.

Qualifications - reasons that someone can accomplish something, usually from previous experience.

Remote - far away and difficult to get to.

Secretary - someone who takes care of personal or business related mail.

Tanzania - a large East African country.

Troop - in biology, the name given to a group of chimpanzees.

Vegetarian - a person or animal who only eats plants or products made from plants.